Anonymous

Minutes of the Fifty-Second Annual Convention of the Evanglical Lutheran Synod and Ministerium of South Carolina and Adjacent States Convened at St. Stephen's Church in Lexington

Anonymous

Minutes of the Fifty-Second Annual Convention of the Evanglical Lutheran Synod and Ministerium of South Carolina and Adjacent States Convened at St. Stephen's Church in Lexington

ISBN/EAN: 9783337226220

Printed in Europe, USA, Canada, Australia, Japan

Cover: Foto ©Lupo / pixelio.de

More available books at **www.hansebooks.com**

MINUTES

OF THE

FIFTY-SECOND ANNUAL CONVENTION

OF THE

Evangelical Lutheran Synod

AND

MINISTERIUM

OF

SOUTH CAROLINA & ADJACENT STATES,

CONVENED AT

ST. STEPHEN'S CHURCH, LEXINGTON CO., S. C.

OCTOBER 10–15, 1876.

THE FIFTY-THIRD ANNUAL CONVENTION OF THE SYNOD OF SOUTH CAROLINA WILL
BE HELD IN ST. MATHEW'S LUTHERAN CHURCH, ORANGEBURG
COUNTY, S. C., BEGINNING ON TUESDAY BEFORE THE
THIRD LORD'S DAY IN OCTOBER, 1877.

CHARLESTON, S. C.
LUCAS & RICHARDSON, PRINT, 66 EAST BAY.
1876.

MINUTES OF SYNOD.

——o——

Sᴛ. STEPHEN'S CHURCH, }
Lᴇxɪɴɢᴛᴏɴ O. H., S. C., October 10th, 1876. }

Pursuant to adjournment, the Eᴠᴀɴɢᴇʟɪᴄᴀʟ Lᴜᴛʜᴇʀᴀɴ Sʏɴᴏᴅ of South Carolina, and adjacent States, met in St. Stephen's Church, Lexington County, S. C., on Thursday, Oct. 14th, 1876, and began the sessions of its *Fifty-Second* Annual Convention.

———

FIRST SESSION.

11 O'ᴄʟᴏᴄᴋ, ᴀ. ᴍ.

Synod was opened by the President, according to our established order. The Secretary called the roll, when the following registry was made :

MINISTERS.	WHEN ENTERED.	POSTOFFICE.
Rev. J. H. Hᴏɴᴏᴜʀ	1834	Charleston, S. C.
" E. A. Bᴏʟʟᴇs	1835	Columbia, S. C.
" D. P. Cᴀᴍᴍᴀɴ*	1835	Troy, Ill.
" E. Cᴀᴜɢʜᴍᴀɴ	1842	Leesville, S. C.
" C. F. Bᴀɴsᴇᴍᴇʀ*	1842	Savannah, Ga.
" D. Sʜᴇᴀʟʏ	1844	Spring Hill, S. C.
" J. H. Bᴀɪʟᴇʏ	1846	Lexington, S. C.
" E. Lᴜғғᴇʀᴅ†	1848	Fort Motte, S. C.
" J. P. Sᴍᴇʟᴛᴢᴇʀ, D D.	1848	Walhalla, S. C.
" J. F. Pʀᴏʙsᴛ	1851	Walhalla, S. C.
" J. H. W. Wᴇʀᴛᴢ	1852	Fort Motte, S. C.
" B. F. Bᴇʀʀʏ	1854	Midway, S. C.
" J. Hᴀᴡᴋɪɴs	1855	Columbia, S. C.

*Absent and excused.
†Absent not excused.

MINISTERS.	WHEN ENTERED.	POSTOFFICE.
Rev. W. S. Bowman, D. D.	1856	Charleston, S. C.
" A. W. Lindler	1856	Leesville, S. C.
" P. Derrick*	1858	Leesville, S. C.
" H. W. Kuhns	1858	Newberry, S. C.
" B. Kreps	1860	Midway, S. C.
" J. D. Bowles	1861	Prosperity, S. C.
" J. D. Shirey	1861	Newberry, S. C.
" J. A. Sligh	1863	Prosperity, S. C.
" A. D. L. Moser	1863	Prosperity, S. C.
" G. W. Holland*	1864	Walhalla, S. C.
" D. Kyzer	1866	Lexington, S. C.
" S. T. Hallman	1868	Orangeburg, S. C.
" H. S. Wingard	1870	Prosperity, S. C.
" C. P. Boozer	1871	Leesville, S. C.
" G. A. Hough	1871	Columbia, S. C.
" Z. W. Bedenbaugh	1874	Prosperity, S. C.
" S. S. Rahn*	1874	Pomaria, S. C.
" J. B. Haskell	1875	Orangeburg, S. C.
" S. P. Hughes‡	1876	Midway, S. C.

LAY DELEGATES.	POSTOFFICE.
J. W. Dreher	Columbia, S. C.
J. M. Weeks	Fort Motte, S. C.
G. T. Berg	Columbia, S. C.
B. Rawl	Rocky Well, S. C.
A. C. Moyer	Ridge Spring, S. C.
A. T. Younginer	Lexington, S. C.
J. D. Shealy	Pomaria, S. C.
E. Crout	Leesville, S. C.
Capt. D. G. Wayne	Charleston, S. C.
J. L. Rast	Orangeburg, S. C.
T. J. Boozer	Prosperity, S. C.
W. H. Dickert	Newberry, S. C.
H. W. Ricard	Newberry, S. C.
Thos. W. Blease†	Johnston, S. C.

*Absent and excused.
‡Ordained at present meeting.
†Absent not excused.

LAY DELEGATES.	POSTOFFICE.
A. H. Wheeler	Prosperity, S. C.
Dr. G. Muller	Sandy Run.
Prof. Auton Berg	Orangeburg, S. C.
C. Ehrhardt	Midway, S. C.

MEMBERS EX-OFFICIO.

Major P. E. Wise	Treasurer of Synod.
Mr. J. F. Schirmer	Treasurer of Seminary Fund.
" U. B. Whites	Treasurer of Missionary Fund.
" O. L. Schumpert	Treasurer of Endowment Fund.

The President then read his Annual Report, which was received, and laid on the table, for reference to the proper Committee:

PRESIDENT'S REPORT.

Beloved Brethren: The Lord has mercifully spared us, to meet again in Synodical Convention. During the year that has past since we last met in this interesting capacity, many changes have taken place—some of a pleasing, and some of a mournful nature. This indeed has been a year always to be remembered in the annals of time, as one of financial pressure, felt, not only by one class or nation, but universally felt throughout the world.

Our own people have been put to no little inconvenience, and many have been crippled in their trade, commerce, and pursuits; consequently the Church feels, and sadly feels, the results of such a pressure. Yet the Lord has been merciful in blessing our land with fruitful seasons, and an abundant harvest. Therefore in view of the multiplied favors and blessings, so richly confered upon us by the "Father of mercies," we would render thanks-giving and praise unto Him, and say, "How great is thy goodness which thou hast wrought for them that trust in Thee." "Thou crownest the year with thy goodness, and thy paths drop fatness."

But while we thus adore and bless the name of our God for His goodness, we should not forget, that one of our number who was wont to meet with us on occasions like the present, is no longer among us. The Rev. S. Bouknight, our esteemed and beloved brother in the Lord; ceased to be mortal on 30th of June, 1876. This Body, by which he was ordained, and in which he spent his whole ministerial life, will not fail to pass suitable resolutions to the memory of a brother so eminently useful, and universally beloved.

Through the *Lutheran Visitor*, and from letters received from some of the brethren, we have learned that a goodly number of our Congregations have been revived and additions made to their membership. Betheny Church in Lexington County, S. C., was dedicated on the 31st October, 1875. This Congregation was formerly received into Synod as Congaree Society.

We also learn that St. Matthew's Church, Orangeburg County, S. C., was repaired, and beautified, and re-dedicated on the 19th March, 1876; and that of St. Matthew's Church, Newberry County, S. C., on the————

My official acts are as follows:

I.—OFFICIAL ACTS.

1. The Rev. G. A. Hough, informed me by a letter, dated Dec. 5th, 1875, that he had received and accepted a call from the Congregation of St. John's Church, Calk's road, Lexington County, S. C., and would enter upon his labors on the fourth Lord's day of the same month.

2. In a letter bearing date January 4th, 1876, Rev. A. W. Lindler, informed me, that notwithstanding the election of Rev. G. A. Hough as Pastor of St. John's Church, that he still retained that relationship to the Church himself, and that his rights and interest had been interfered with by that brother.

3. Shortly after the reception of the above letter, I received one from Rev. G. A. Hough, requesting me in the name of the Congregation of St. John's to install him as their Pastor, on the third Sabbath in January, 1876. In compliance with this request, I went to the Church at the appointed time, and after having fully satisfied myself that Rev. G. A. Hough was the duly elected Pastor, I proceeded to install him as such, in the presence of Rev. A. W. Lindler, and the Congregation. As there has a difficulty grown out of my action in regard to this affair, I herewith submit a statement of the whole matter, together with some written testimony, and I ask for myself and others, that this Body examine the same, and in its decision to give no uncertain sound, whether for or against me, that your presiding officer and others, may hereafter know how to proceed with such cases.

4. In a letter bearing date January 1st, 1876, Rev. B. F. Berry, asked permission to preach to some scattered members of our Church, living at, and in the vicinity of Allendale, S. C., on the Port Royal Railroad, I complied with his wishes and incouraged him in the work.

5. In January, 1876, I received letters from Revs. E. Caughman and D. Shealy, and from the Church Council of Good Hope Church, Edgefield County, S. C., in reference to supplying Pastorate No. 6, with preaching. After prayerfully considering the matter, I concluded to comply with the wishes of the Congregations, comprisng said Pastorate, and allowed Rev. E. Caughman to supply

God Hope Church, and Rev. D. Shealy, Union and Salem. This charge is still without a Pastor.

6. Rev. J. Hawkens took charge of Pastorate No. 9, on the 20th of April last, and on the 15th of June, he handed me a certificate of honorable dismissure from the Maryland Synod, signed by its President, the Rev. W. S. Owen. Rev. Hawkins is accordingly a member of Synod. On the 30th of May, in Bethel Church, Lexington County, S. C., in the presence of a large Congregation, he was installed Pastor of the charge.

7. In May last, I received a letter from Rev. T. W. Dosh, D. D., asking for an honorable dismissure from this Body, to the Evangelical Lutheran Synod of North Carolina. I sent him the desired paper.

8. At the request of the members of the Board of Trustees and Faculty of Newberry College, together with other Members of Synod and Members of our Church, I called a Church Convention, which convened at Bethlehem Church, Newberry County, S. C., on the 12th July, 1876. The object of the Convention was to consider the Bachman Endowment. At this meeting the action of the Faculty in appointing Mr. S. D. Hughes as the Agent for the collection of funds for the Endowment was endorsed, and a plan for raising a sufficient amount was adopted. Mr. Hughes has not as yet entered upon his labors, but we learn that he will do so in a short time.

9. Rev. E. A. Wingard, in September last, requested me by letter, to send him a certificate of dismissal from this Synod to the North Carolina Synod. I did as requested.

10. I received on the 10th August, 1876, from Rev. C. P. Boozer a certificate signed by Rev. J. P. Margart, the President of the Georgia Synod, dismissing him from that Body to this. He is therefore a member of Synod, and was installed by Rev. H. S. Wingard, Pastor of Pastorate No. 7, at Corinth Church, Edgefield County, S. C., on the 24th September, 1876.

11. The Rev. H. S. Wingard informed me in September last, that he had resigned his charge; but we have since leaned that his people are making an effort to have him continue with them. This is as it ought to be, as too frequent changes in the pastoral work benefit neither people nor Pastor.

12. I received September 8th, a letter from Rev. J. H. Bailey who was appointed by the Edgefield Conference to lay before me, as President of Synod, the destitute condition of many of the Churches belonging to said Conference, and the importance of something being speedily done for their relief. I herewith submit to Synod for its action, that part of Brother Bailey's letter which looks to an increase in the ministry by adopting what is known as the Home Student System.

13. The Rev. S. S. Rahn informed me by letter dated Sept. 23d, 1876, that he had resigned one of the Churches composing his charge, and that he intended to resign the other at his next appointment.

14. At the instance of several clerical members of Synod, I appointed on the 4th inst., Rev. Prof. J. P. Smeltzer, D. D., Corresponding Delegate to the Tennesee Synod, which convened at St. John's Church, Lexington Connty, S. C., on the 5th of October, 1876. This important matter it seems, was overlooked at our last annual meeting, and as great good to the Church might grow out of an interchange of delegates, between the two bodies, and having some constitutional grounds for believing that I had the power to make the appointment, I did so, with the hope, that it might meet with your approval.

15. On the 4th inst., I received a communication from Rev. D. P. Camman, of Troy, Illinois, asking to be excused for non-attendance at our present Convention, and requesting an honorable dismission from this Body. As the meeting of Synod was so near at hand, and as Brother Camman does not give the name of Synod with which he wishes to unite, I thought it best to put the letter into the hands of Synod, and accordingly herewith submit it.

RECOMMENDATIONS.

I. THEOLOGICAL SEMINARY.

The Rev. J. F. Campbell, President of the Board of Directors of the Theological Seminary, in accordance with the resolution adopted at the late meeting of the Virginia Synod, and by the authority given him by the General Synod, calls the attention of this Body to the necessity of nominating the First Chair in the Seminary, viz: that of Systematic and Practical Theology, at its present meeting. I therefore recommend, that Synod make said nomination.

II.—NEWBERRY COLLEGE.

Your President is the Secretary of the Board of Trustees of Newberry College. For information on this important subject, I refer you to his report. I herewith submit a copy of an Assignment of claims against Newberry College made by John P. Kinard and W. A. Cline to the South Carolina Synod.

III.—BIBLE CAUSE.

The Rev. Edwin A. Bolles, who has for twenty-five years been successfully engaged in the distribution of the Holy Bible, notified me in a letter dated June 12th, 1876, that he had on that day tendered the resignation of his office as District Superintendent America Bible Society for South Carolina, to take effect on the first of October next, and that he desired to spend the remainder of his life as Pastor of a Lutheran Congregation or Congregations. Our

Protestant Churches of all denominations owe a debt of gratitude to Bro. Bolles, for so faithfully spreading the word of God throughout the length and breadth of our State; and our Evangelical. Lutheran Church, and more especially our Synod, should exert itself in his behalf to secure him a field of labor.

As this Body year after year has endorsed Brother Bolles, and the good work in which he has been engaged, we should now assure the American Bible Society that our love for, and interest in it, does not cease with the retirement of our Brother, but that we shall continue to co-operate with it in the dissemination of God's word.

IV.—CONFERENCES.

The Churches belonging to the Edgefield Conference, are many of them now in a languishing condition, and it is apprehended that further injury may come upon them, if something is not speedily done in the way of throwing more Ministers into that Conference. I therefore recommend that Synod designate and establish a dividing line between the Newberry and Edgefield Conferences, so as to give from the former to the latter Conference several of its active and efficient clerical members with their Congregations.

V—PASTORATES.

As a number of changes, in order to give satisfaction, has already been made by Synod in some of the Pastoral Districts in Edgefield and Lexington Counties, and as petitions from some of these very same Churches are annually sent up to this Body, and applications made to the President in the *interim* of Synod to make other changes, and allow individual Congregations to make their own arrangements for preaching, it would seem that a good deal of dissatisfaction still exists among those charges; therefore, on this account, and knowing how difficult it is for Synod in such matters, through a Committee, to get at the true state of affairs, I recommend that in case a boundary line be fixed between the Newberry and Edgefield Conferences, that the President of Synod call a meeting of the Conference or Conferences to which said Churches may belong, to convene soon after the rising of Synod, and that he, the President, attend such meeting or meetings in his official capacity and together with the members of Conference or Conferences make, if posible, such arrangements in Districting the Churches, as will give satisfaction and render them more efficient in the future. and that the action taken go into immediate effect, but be subject to the confirmation of Synod.

2

And now dear Brethren, grateful to you for your consideration. I return the trust Committed to me one year ago, back into your hands, praying that God may bless us in our deliberations, in our labor of love, and in every effort that we shall make to extend the borders of our beloved Lutheran Zion.

J. A. SLIGH,
President of the Synod of South Carolina, and Adjacent States.

The annual election for officers was entered into and resulted as follows:

President.—Rev. Edwin A. Bolles.
Vice-President.—Rev. W. S. Bowman, D. D.
Recording Secretary.—Rev. C. P. Boozer.
Corresponding Secretary.—Rev. H. W. Kuhns.
Treasurer of Synod.—Major P. E. Wise.
Treasurer of Seminary Fund.—Mr. J. F. Schirmer.
Treasurer of Missionary Fund.—Mr. U. B. Whites.
Treasurer of Endowment Fund.—Mr. O. L. Schumpert.

The the newly elected officers assumed the duties of their respective seats.

Rev. J. N. Derrick, Corresponding Delegate from the Georgia Synod, was introduced and received as a member of Synod, upon which he presented the fraternal greeting of the Synod to which he belongs, when the President of Synod, in suitable terms responded.

Then, a resolution was adopted that Rev. Dr. Dosh, of North Carolina Synod, be received as an advisory member.

Letters and documents intended for Synod were now called for to be placed in the hands of the proper Committees.

Synod adjourned for one hour.

Prayer by Rev. H. W. Kuhns.

AFTERNOON SESSION.

2 O'CLOCK, P. M.

Synod reassembled, and was opened with prayer by Rev. J. N. Derrick.

The President announced the following Standing Committees:

1. *Committee on President's Report.*—Revs. J. Hawkins, J. H. Bailey, and Mr. J. W. Dreher.

2. *Minutes of last Synod.*—Revs. J. D. Bowles, A. W. Lindler, and Mr. U. B. Whites.

3. *Letters and Excuses.*—Revs. J. B. Haskell, E. Caughman, and Mr. A. I. Younginer.

4. *On State of Religion.*—Revs. J. F. Probst, J. A. Sligh, and Capt. D. G. Wayne.

5. *On Report of Treasurer of Synod.*—Messrs. U. B. Whites, James Rast, and T. J. Boozer.

6. *On Treasurer of Seminary Fund.*—Messrs. G. T. Berg, W. H. Dickert, and Col. O. L. Schumpert.

7. *On Treasurer of Missionary Fund.*—Messrs. J. F. Schirmer, Benjamin Rawl, and Ephraim Crout.

8. *On Treasurer of Endowment Fund.*—Dr. G. Muller, A. H. Wheeler, and Major P. E. Wise.

9. *On Treasurer of Widow's Fund.*—Col. O. L. Schumpert, Mr. John D. Shealy.

10. *On Pastoral Districts.*—Revs. J. A. Sligh, E. Caughman, and H. S. Wingard.

11. *On Appropriations.*—Revs. J. D. Shirey, Dr. J. P. Smeltzer, and Mr. U. B. Whites.

12. *On Reports of Conference.*—Revs. Dr. J. P. Smeltzer, D. Shealy, and A. D. L. Moser.

———

Rev. J. H. Bailey, Corresponding Delegate to the Georgia Synod, made the following report, which was received and adopted:

REPORT OF THE CORRESPONDING DELEGATE TO THE GEORGIA SYNOD.

Your Delegate begs leave to report, that he attended the Sixteenth Annual Convention of the Evangelical Lutheran Synod of Georgia, and adjacent States, held in Bethel Church, near Springfield, Effingham County, Ga., on Oct., 1875. He was kindly received and tendered to the Brethren composing that Body, the fraternal greetings of this, the mother Synod. It was a meeting of more than ordinary interest. Matters of vital importance to the welfare of the Church in the State of Georgia were freely and fully discussed, and all their deliberations were characterized by a spirit of brotherly love and singular unanimity. These Brethren very wisely resolved to rid themselves of the incumbrance of their Classical School for the present at least, and to concentrate all their available means, their energies and labors, in the single object of missions within their bounds. In pursuance of this purpose they took the initiatory steps to establish, as soon as practicable, a Missionary Station at Atlanta, Ga. In their efforts to build up. Lutheranism at that very important point, your Delegate assured these brethren that they would receive not only the earnest sympathy. but also the hearty co-operation of the South Carolina Synod, who must be equally interested with them in this important enterprise. How far your Delegate was warranted in giving this assurance, will be determined by your action should this subject come properly before you.

My necessary travelling expenses were $13.60.

Respectfully submitted,
JAS. H. BAILEY.

———

Rev. J. P. Smeltzer, D. D., Corresponding Delegate to the Tennesee Synod, made his report, which was received and adopted:

REPORT OF THE CORRESPONDING DELEGATE TO THE TENNESEE SYNOD.

Your Delegate, appointed by the President, to the Tennesee Synod, would report, that he attended to the duty assigned him. That Body met at St. John's Church, Lexington County, Oct. 5th, 1876. Your Delegate was cordially received, and participated in their deliberations. Owing to the great distance many had to travel, and the expense in reaching Synod, many were absent, but those present seemed actively engaged in the work assigned them. At this session they abolished the licensure system, and refused to unite with any of the General Bodies of the Lutheran Church. They appointed a Delegate to attend this session of your Synod, and as this Synod will meet again before their next Convention, they also appointed a Delegate to attend your next Convention.

Respectfully submitted,
J. P. SMELTZER.

———

Rev. E. A. Bolles, Corresponding Delegate to the North Carolina Synod, made a report which was received and adopted:

REPORT OF THE DELEGATE TO THE LUTHERAN SYNOD OF NORTH CAROLINA.

Pursuant to appointment of the Lutheran Synod of South Carolina in the month of October, 1875, I attended as your fraternal Delegate, the Lutheran Synod of North Carolina, during the month of May, 1876. The Rev. S. Rothrock, of the North Carolina Synod. was appointed the fraternal Delegate to attend the present meeting of the South Carolina Synod.

EDWIN A. BOLLES.

The report of the Delegates to the the General Synod was read, and referred to a Special Committee, consisting of the following : Revs. J. P. Smeltzer, D. D., W. S. Bowman, D. D., and J. Hawkins.

The Committee on the Memoirs of Rev. J. B. Lowman and Rev. Samuel Bouknight, now reported, which was received and adopted by a rising vote.

The Parochial Reports and Reports on the State of Religion were then called for, and read by the different Pastors.

Pending the reading of Parochial Reports Synod adjourned to meet to-morrow at 9 o'clock.

Prayer by Rev. T. W. Dosh, D. D.

SECOND SESSION.

WEDNESDAY, OCT. 11TH, 9 O'CLOCK, A. M.

Synod met and was opened with singing, and Prayer by the Rev. J. H. Honour. The Secretary called the roll, and the minutes of yesterday were read and approved.

It was then,

Resolved, That the three front seats of each tier of pews be established as the bar of Synod.

The Secretary of the Board of Trustees of Newberry College read his report, which was referred to a Committee consisting of Revs. J. D. Shirey, J. H. Honour, and Mr. G. T. Berg.

REPORT OF SECRETARY OF THE BOARD OF TRUSTEES OF NEWBERRY COLLEGE.

The College has been in successful operation during the year that closed in June last, the catalogue showing that there were one hundred and one students in attendance. Four young men graduated at last Commencement, and the Commencement exercises were highly encouraging in every particular. The session of the present Collegiate year which opened on the 7th September last, does not speak very encouragingly for the Institution, there being only fifty students up to this time. There is, however, even in this. one encouraging feature, and that is thirty-six of this number are in the Collegiate Department. As the Faculty receives now only what comes in from tuition, without a considerable increase of students, in a short time their salary will be meagre.

At this meeting of Synod the arrangements made with Rev. Prof. J. F. Probts cease—it will be for you to say whether the same or similar arrangements shall be continued. The German language, which should be highly prized by the Evangelical Lutheran Church, is becoming more and more important all over our Country, and if this chair should be discontinued, the College will be crippled to an extent that many now, perhaps little suspect. I therefore recommend that this Body authorize the Board of Trustees to make arrangements with Rev. Prof. Probts for another year.

It is not very encouraging to learn that the town of Walhalla, the place where the College is located, furnishes only twelve students to the Institution. These people have not complied with the conditions made by this Body three years ago to insure to them the permanent location of the College. The tuition in the Preparatory Department has been kept entirely too low in order to please them, and encourage them to patronize the Institution, and withal we get but twelve students. Is not this sufficient evidence to prove that they do not appreciate the Institution?

It is certainly a question of vast importance to our Church whether the time has not come to locate the College at a place where the citizens will generally patronize it, in the centre of the Church, among our own people where they can send their sons to it without incurring so much expense, and when its educational influence would go out to benefit those who support it. As the question of removal is now being agitated in private circles to the present injury of our Professors and College, by causing an uneasiness of feeling among the Students, and by keeping others away, I therefore recommend that this Body say positively that it shall or shall not remain at Walhalla, and if it is concluded to remove it, that we say definitely that the removal shall not take place until a specified time. Such a course on the part of Synod is all important as a whole years agitation will, beyond a doubt, kill the Institution.

In all other respects, except those mentioned above, the College is doing well. By the generous act of Mr. W. A. Cline, Maj. J. P. Kinard, Capt. A. P. Pifer and others, the College is freed from the embarrassment of old debts hanging over it. The kindness of these gentlemen should not be overlooked or forgotten by this Body. Our Professors are faithful in the discharge of their duties, and whenever a young man goes forth with his credentials from the Institution, this itself is evidence that he has been thoroughly trained, and that he is qualified to fill no mean position in Church or State. The number of graduates is increasing annually, and therefore new workers for the Institution are being added to our number every year.

The Board of Trustees during last Commencement week. held an informal meeting, and transacted such business that was obliged to be attended to. Another meeting was called for the 12th of July last at Bethlehem Church, Newberry County, S. C., at which meeting that which had been informally done for the want of a quorum was confirmed. By resolution of the Board, it was made my duty to report the attendance and absence of the members of the Board to this Body. I herewith submit said report, which ought to be placed into the hands of the Committee appointed to nominate members of the Board.

We now have greater hopes of the prosperity of the College than at any previous period for the last twelve years. The hardest work has been done, and the greatest difficulties overcome. Let the agent for the Endowment go to work with a determination to succeed, let our people and the friends of the College rally one time more, and let us at our present Convention, act judiciously in the affairs of the Institution, and victory will perch upon our banner, and Newberry College will live to do a great and glorious work for our Church and Country.

J. A. SLIGH,

Secretary of Board of Trustees.

Rev. H. S. Wingard was appointed Assistant Secretary of Synod. Then O. L. Schumpert, Esq., Chairman of the Committee on pecuniary affairs of Newberry College, read their report.

The undersigned Committee, appointed under, and by virtue of a resolution passed at the last Synod of our Church, pages 25 and 26, relative to the pecuniary difficulties incompassing Newberry College, with full authority to said Committee, to take such steps as shall honorably relieve said Institution, of all its liabilities, beg leave to report:

Your Committee has attained releases and assignments of the following claims, which were established against said Institution. in the case of Jos. A. and R. H. Man. Executors, &c., *vs.* J. P. Kinard, and Trustees of Newberry College, to wit:

Claim of J. P. Kinard, exclusive of interest				....	$13,700.00
" " W. A. Cline,	"	"	"	....	3,800.00
" " A. P. Pifer,	"	"	"	....	1,644.65
" " Wm. Johnson,	"	"	"	....	36.00

$19,180.65

Making a total, which has been released and assigned, of Nineteen Thousand One Hundred and Eighty Dollars, and Sixty-five Cents. Out side of said case, your Committee has also obtained a release and assignment of the only other debt against said Institution, or the Trustees thereof, to wit: Claim of J. P. Aull, contracted in 186 $300.00.

The release and assignment of said Claims, is in writing under the hand and seal of the several Creditors, the originals of which are of record in the office of Register of Mesne Conveyance, for Newberry County, State of South Carolina, and on file in the above stated case.   Certified copies of said assignments are now in poses-sion of the President of Synod.

Thus Newberry College, by one stroke, has been released of all her pecuniary liabilities past and present; and with this relief, your Committee sincerely trust. has also vanished forever the great bug-bear, which has ever stood as an insurmountable obstacle in the path of those who would have rallied to her succor in' the times of dire need.

Respectfully, submitted,

O. L. SCUMPERT, *Chairman.*
H. W. KUHNS,
J. A. SLIGH.

Which was referred with accompanying documents to the Committee on Secretary's Report.   Also, the Report of the Committee which was appointed to secure an Agent to prosecute the Endowment Fund, was received and referred to the same Committee.

THE REPORT OF THE COMMITTEE TO SECURE AN AGENT TO PROSECUTE THE ENDOWENT FUND.

Your Committee, appointed at the last meeting of Synod, to secure an agent to complete the Bachman Endowment Fund of Newberry College, would submit the following report, viz:

As soon as possible, after Synod adjourned, the Agency was offered to Rev. H. W. Kuhns, who declined serving on account of his health, and other reasons.   We then endeavored to secure the services of Rev. H. S. Wingard, and we were making arrangements to enable him to enter upon the work; but he finally declined serving.   The Committee then endeavored to secure the President of College as Agent, who, on account of serious illness in his family, and believing that he was not the right man to succeed in the work, refused to accept the Agency.   The Agency was then offered to Mr. S. P. Hughes.   Mr. Hughes consented to serve for a salary of $1,000, he defraying all expenses and securing the same from the cash subscriptions. Mr. Hughes was unable to commence the work on account of his health, until the present meeting of Synod.

As nothing has been done in securing the completion of the Endowment fund, your Committee return the trust to the Synod, and ask to be discharged.

Respectfully submitted,

J. P. SMELTZER,
Chairman of Faculty of Newberry College.

Mr. S. P. Hughes, Theological Student, was received as an advisory member of Synod.

The reading of Parochial Reports was resumed.

Synod adjourned for divine service; benediction by Rev. J. H. Bailey.

The Synodical sermon was preached by the retiring President, Rev. J. A. Sligh, from Rev. II., 1–6.

AFTERNOON SESSION.

2 O'CLOCK, P. M.

Synod was called to order by the President, and opened with prayer by Rev. A. W. Lindler.

It was then,

Resolved, That it is the understanding of this Synod that authority was given at our last annual meeting to the Faculty of Newberry College to employ an Agent to canvass the field in behalf of the Bachman Endowment.

Rev. D. Efird, presented his credentials, and was received as the Corresponding Delegate from the Evangelical Lutheran Tennessee Synod.

On taking his seat he made some appropriate remarks tendering the fraternal greetings of his Synod, which were responded to by the President.

The Rev. T. J. Clyde, of the M. E. Church South, was received as an advisory member of this Body.

The Committee on the President's Report, reported as follows which was received and considered by items:

3

42450

REPORT OF COMMITTEE ON PRESIDENT'S ADDRESS.

Your Committee unite with the retiring President in thanksgiving to Almighty God, for the blessings of his hand vouch-safed to us as a Synod during the year.

Matters of a grave and important character have claimed the attention of the President, requiring wise counsel and sound judgment, and we are happy to record the fact, that he has acted very judiciously, and we hope for the best interest of our Zion in every instance.

1. In regard to the difficulties between the President and Rev. A. W. Lindler, arising from the installation of Rev. G. A. Hough, as Pastor of St. John's, your Committee, after carefully examining the testimony submitted by the President and the Officers of St. John's Church, are of opinion, that the President acted in accordance with constitutional law and order; but that Synod may have a fair opportunity of judging in the matter, and fixing a precedent for our guidance in the future, as the President suggests, we respectfully refer this part of the report to the Synod for its investigation.

2. The calling of the Convention in July last, by the President, meets with our entire approbation, and we are happy to learn that the health of the Agent, appointed by the faculty of Newberry College, is so much improved, that he will be able soon to enter upon his Agency.

3. The letter referred to by the President, in regard to the destitution in portions of our Church, together with a memorial, signed by two hundred and fifteen members of our Church within the bounds of the Third Conference, laying before Synod their destitution, and praying for the re-establishing of what is known as the Home Student System, or some other plan by which the number of our working ministry may be increased, without incurring the heavy expense and tardy process of a collegiate and thorough theological training, is a matter of too grave importance and vital interest to our Church, to be passed over without receiving the most serious and prayerful attention of this Body. We therefore suggest the adoption of the following:

1. That we adhere strictly to the high standard of training now in use in our Institutions, in every case where it is practicable, and that no exceptions be made, except in extreme cases; for which provision is already made in the constitution.

2. The President refers to the case of Rev. D. P. Camman. We think he acted wisely in not granting his dismission, as no Synod with which he proposed to connect himself was designated. We recommend that the Corresponding Secretary be required to inform Brother Camman, that his request shall be granted so soon as he designates the Synod with which he proposes to connect himself.

3. As the matter of Newberry College referred to in the report, will come before Synod through Committees, we have nothing to suggest. .

4. We take pleasure in re-affirming what the President says in regard to the efficiency of Rev. E. A. Bolles, as General Agent of the A. B. Society for S. C., and of our continued interest in the Bible Cause; and we earnestly hope to have the pleasure very soon, of seeing Brother Bolles comfortably located in some pleasant charge within our bounds.

5. The matter of a re-division of our conferences, is of vital importance to portions of our Church, and your Committee recommend that a line be so established between the Newberry and Edgefield Conferences, as to throw two or three more Pastorates into the Edgefield Conference.

6. We recommend that the plan suggested by the President, in regard to Pastoral Districts, be adopted and acted upon, as soon after the rising of Synod as practicable.

J. HAWKINS.
J. H. BAILEY.
J. W. DREHER.

Item I. Adopted.

Item II. Adopted.

Synod entered upon the investigation referred to in the second item of the above report, having first sought Divine guidance in prayer by Rev. W. S. Bowman, D. D. .

After a protracted discussion, a resolution was offered, that the President be sustained in his action noticed in item the second.

Item III. Pending the consideration of this item of the Report, Synod adjourned to meet in Ministerium.

Prayer by Rev. J. H. W. Wertz.

Preaching at night in the Church by Rev. J. B. Haskell, from Rev. 3: 11.

THIRD SESSION.

THURSDAY, OCT. 12TH, 9 O'CLOCK, A. M.

Synod convened and was opened with prayer by Rev. E. Caughman.

The Roll was called, and dates of entering the Ministry. and Postoffice addresses of Ministers were corrected.

Rev. B. F. Berry and Mr. C. Ehrhardt, appeared and were received as members of Synod.

The minutes were read and approved.

A letter from the Pastor of the A. M. E. Church was read, requesting that his pulpit be filled by members of Synod during this Convention.

Referred to Committee on Divine Service.

The business of this hour was read and considered.

Item III.   Amended and adopted.

Item IV.   Adopted.

Item V.   Adopted.

Item VI.   Adopted.

Item VII.   Adopted.

When it was,

Resolved, That the Committee on the President's Report, be appointed a Committee to make the boundary line of Conference, and report at this meeting of Synod.

Item VIII.   Adopted.

The report adopted as a whole.

The Report of the Corresponding Secretary was read, adopted, and referred to the following Committee: Revs. W. S. Bowman, J. H. Honour, and Mr. U. B. Whites.

REPORT OF CORRESPONDING SECRETARY.

Your Corresponding Secretary would report the following, viz:

1. The letter of Mr. Whittle, referred to me at the last Convention of Synod, with a view of further correspondence, was not answered till the 18th January. This delay was occasioned by a diligent, but fruitless search for the obligations of this renegade. Finding it impossible to lay hands upon said obligations, if any are in existence, by correspondence with Mr. J. F. Schirmer, I learned that, according to the showing of the Minutes, Mr. Whittle's indebtedness to Synod, is two hundred and six dollars ($206.25) and twenty-five cents.

When this information was received, I wrote to Mr. Whittle, urging him to refund. But having heard nothing from him up to the 7th ult., I again addressed him on the same subject. To this letter an answer was received recently, which is herewith submitted.

2. I also wrote to four other individuals, who I was informed, were formerly beneficiaries of this Body; but only one of these answered my letters; and he claimed that he owed Synod nothing.

3. Jan. 5th, I received a letter from Rev. Kuhns, addressed to Dr. Dosh by Rev. J. B. Reimensnyder relative to the Atlanta Mission. Also one from Rev. J. F. Probst, (6th February) on the same subject. Brother Kuhns answered the former one of these letters requesting more light on the subject; but as neither he nor I received any further information relative to this matter, no action was taken. These letters are herewith submitted.

4. I sent a copy of our minutes to the Secretaries of Virginia, North Carolina, Tennessee, and Georgia Synods, and the Constitutional number to the Secretary of our General Synod.

5. The only minutes received were those of Georgia Synod. This Synod numbers 10 Ministers; 13 Congregations, and 1,132 Communicants.

There has been no meeting of the Executive Committee during the Synodical year. As your Superintendent of Home Missions was employed by Synod, he has made no report to the Executive Committee; but it is presumed that he will report to this Body.

Respectfully submitted,

J. D. SHIREY, C. S.

Synod adjourned for Divine service.

Benediction by Rev. D. Shealy.

Sermon by Rev. J. D. Shirey, from St. John XV: 5.

AFTERNOON SESSION.

2 o'clock, P. M.

Synod was called to order by the President, and opened with prayer by Rev. D. Shealy.

The report of the Committee on the report of the Board of Trustees of Newberry College and other papers, were taken up, received, and adopted by items:

REPORT OF SPECIAL COMMITTEE.

The papers referred to your Committee are ;

I. The Report of Secretary of the Board of Trustees of Newberry College.

1. The first item in this Report claiming your attention is the expiration of the time for which arrangements were made with Rev. Probst as Professor of the German Language in Newberry College.

In reference to this matter, we recommend that Synod make arrangements, similar to those of last year, with Prof. Probst.

2. The second item alluded to is that of another location of the Institution. In reference to this important matter, we offer the following :

Whereas. The citizens of Walhalla and vicinity, have failed to comply with the terms proposed by this Body three years ago, for the permanent location of Newberry College in their midst, and

Whereas, They fail to manifest such an appreciation of said In-stitution, as warants us to believe that its permanent location at Walhalla would be compatible with our deliberate judgment, therefore

a. Resolved, That we invite bids for the permanent location of Newberry College, from any city or town that may desire the per-manent location of a literary Institution in its midst, and that a Committee be charged with the publication of this matter, and the reception of such bids, to be submitted to this Body at such time as it shall hereafter designate.

b. Resolved, That the time for the reception of such bids be extended to 2d April, 1877, and that this Body convene on the 3d day of April, 1877, at such place as the Committee shall designate for the purpose of considering any and all bids, or propositions of any kind, that may then be made for, and in consideration of the permanent location of Newberry College, and any other matters relating to the College that may demand its attention.

c. Resolved, That the Institution be continued at Walhalla till the expiration of the present scholastic year.

3. We recommend the adoption of the Report.

II. The next paper in our hands is the Report of the Committee appointed at last meeting of Synod, to take such steps as would honorably releive Newberry College of all its liabilities, together with duplicate copies of releases and assignments of certain claim-ants against the Institution.

1. We recommend the adoption of this Report.

2. We recommend that one copy each of the aforesaid releases and assignments be placed in the archives of Synod, and that the other copy of each be placed in the archives of the College.

3. In attestation of our appreciation of the generosity of Mr. W. A. Cline, Maj. Kinard, Capt. Pifer, Capt. Aull and Mr. Johnson, in the relinquishment of their claims upon the Institu-tion, and also to Mr. H. C. Moses for gratuitously recording the aforesaid papers.

We recommend that the Corresponding Secretary in the name of Synod, be authorized to assure each of these parties of our grati-tude for their favors, thus bestowed upon this Body and its Institution.

4. We recommend a vote of thanks to the Committee for their interest in, labor and success in this matter.

III. The third document in our hands is a Report of the Faculty of Newberry College, charged with the appointment of an Agent for the Bachman Endowment. We recommend,

1. That the Report be adopted.

2. That we endorse the action of the Faculty in the appointment of Brother Hughes as Agent for the Bachman Endowment, and pledge him our co-operation in the work entrusted to him.

Respectfully submitted,

J. D. SHIREY,
JNO. H. HONOUR.
G. T. BERG.

First item. Adopted.
Second item. Referred for action to-morrow afternoon.
Third item. Adopted.
Fourth item. Adopted.
Fifth item. Adopted.
Sixth item. Adopted.
Seventh item. Adopted.
Eighth item. Adopted.

The report of the Committee on the report of the Treasurer of Seminary Fund, was read and adopted :

LEXINGTON, C. H., Nov. 12th, 1876.

Your Committee to whom was referred the Accounts of the Treasurer of the Theological Seminary, have examined the same, find them correct, and properly vouched for. Our venerable Treasurer has a balance of $1,077 31 on hand, which owing to the great difficulty of finding a safe investment, bear as yet no interest; but on his return home, he thinks to accomplish his aim, that the funds of the Seminary should produce the " ten talents."

Your Committee can indeed pronounce his accounts as *correct*, in as much as according to a resolution passed at the last Synodical Convention, page 29, the Treasurer brings a certificate that the assets are on hand.   Respectfully submitted,

G. T. BERG, *Chairman*,
O. L. SCHUMPERT.

JACOB F. SCHIRMER, TREASURER, IN ACCOUNT WITH THEOLOGICAL SEMINARY.

1875.   Dr.

October—Balance in hand as per acct. current this date..	$255	31
1876.		
April—Received one year's interest on S. C. R. R. Bonds.	280	00
May — Received one year's interest on Bond of $2,000..	160	00
" Received one year's interest on Bond of $1,400..	140	00
April—Received ¾ interest on City Stock, less tax......	22	50
" Received interest on Bond of $810 in full to February last...............................	130	00
June—Received interest on Bond of $2,700 to May last....................................	270	00
July—Received one year's interest on Five shares Bank of Charleston...........................	30	00
" Received one year's interest on Two shares Union Bank..................................	6	00
Jan.—Received ½ year's interest on Forty shares Gas Company................................	40	00
July—Received ¼ year's interest on Forty-six shares Gas Company................................	34	50
July—One year's interest on one Atlanta Bond (less ex).	79	00
July—One year's interest on Fire Loan Bonds.........	203	00
August—One year's int. on Bond of $750 to March last..	75	00
September—One year's interest on N. E. R. R. Bond....	120	00
	$1,845	31

1875.   Cr.

November—Paid Rev. Repass 1 qrs. salary & ex.	$125	50
" Paid quota of repairs to Seminary Building......................	15	00
1876.		
February—Paid for six shares Gas Co. Stock...	150	00
" Paid Rev. Repass 1 qrs. salary and expenses......................	125	50
May—Paid Rev. Repass 1 qrs. salary and expenses..................................	125	50
August—Paid Rev. Repass 1 qrs. salary and expenses..................................	125	50
August—Paid for one Non-Taxable Bond of $100..............................	86	00
October—Incidental Expenses past year........	15	00
Balance in hand of Treasurer.......	$1,077	31
	$1,845	31

ASSETS OF FUNDS OF SEMINARY.

One Personal Bond for $2,000 at 8 per ct......................
   "   "   1,400 at 10..........................
   "   "   2,700 at 10..........................
   "   "   861 at 12..........................
   "   "   750 at 10..........................
   "   "   250 at 10..........................
One note with collaterals, 500 at 8..........................
Eight (8) S. C. R R. Bond at $500..........................
Five (5) Fire Loan Bonds at 500..................... ....
Four (4)   "   "   at 100..............................
Three (3) N. E. R. R. Bonds at 500..........................
One Atlanta Bond at 1,000..................................
One non-taxable Bond at 100................................
Certificates of City Stock at 650..........................
Forty-six (46) shares in Gas Company.......................
Five (5) shares Bank of Charleston.........................
Two (2) shares Union Bank..................................

CHARLESTON, S. C., October 6th, 1876.

We do hereby certify that the above Bonds and specialties were produced to us by the Treasurer, and examined and found all correct.   F. C. BLUM.
                             JOHN KLINCK.

The Committee on Letters and Petitions made the following report, which was received and considered by items:

REPORT ON LETTERS.

Your Committee on Letters, beg leave to report as follows:

Letter No. 1.—From Rev. A. R. Rude. Recommend that it be received and read by Synod.

Letter No. 2.—Excuse from Rev. G. W. Holland. We recommend it be received and read by Synod.

Letter No. 3.—From Rev. D. P. Camman. We recommend it be read and request granted.

Letter No. 4.—From Rev. S. Rothrock, Delegate from N. C. Synod. Your Committee recommend: 1st. That it be received and read before Synod. 2d. That in accordance with the wish therein expressed, a Delegate be appointed or elected to N. C. Synod.

4

Letter No. 5.—Memorial from Mt. Calvary Church. Edgefield County. Your Committee recommend that the Corresponding Secretary be instructed to communicate with the Elders and Deacons of Mt. Calvary Church, and refer them to part 2, Art. 11 of the Constitution and By-Laws of the Evangelical Lutheran Synod of South Carolina, and recommend them earnestly to use every endeavor to give the young men referred to, a Collegiate education. In cases where this is impossible, the young men should make individual application to Synod.

Letter No. 6.—Memorial from Orangeburg Conference. Recommend it be read and referred to Committee on Conferences.

Letter No. 7.—Invitation from St. Matthew's Evangelical Lutheran Church, Orangeburg County, extended to Synod, praying that the next meeting be held in their Church. Which Letter your Committee return to Synod for action.

Letter No. 8.—From Rev. S. S. Rahn. Committee recommend he be excused.

Letter No. 9.—Verbally reported by Rev. E. Caughman, who has letter, being an excuse for Rev. Paul Derrick. Recommend it be granted.

Respectfully submitted,
J. BACHMAN HASKELL.
E. CAUGHMAN.
A. J. YOUNGINGER.

Item 1. Adopted, and Rev. A. R. Rude, D. D., excused.

Item 2. Adopted, and Rev. G. W. Holland, excused.

Item 3. Adopted, and Rev. D. P. Camman, excused.

Item 4. Adopted.

Under this item, the following was adopted:

Resolved, That we accept the excuse of Rev. Rothrock, Corresponding Delegate elect from North Carolina Synod, and regret the circumstances which prevent his presence with us. And that we rejoice in the prospect of a union of the Synod which he represents with the Evangelical Lutheran General Synod in North America.

Item 5. Recommitted with instructions.

Item 6. Referred to Committee on Conferences.

Item 7. Adopted.

Item 8. Adopted.

Item 9. Adopted.

The following amendments to Constitution of Synod were made and adopted:

Having given notice a year ago, according to the requirements of the Constitution, for an amendment to Art. 5th, Chap. 14th of the Constitution of Synod, therefore,

Resolved, That the following addition be made to said article: " But should he continue faithful in the discharge of his dutie;, as a Lutheran Minister for *ten years*, his obligations shall be cancelled and his bonds returned to him."

Also, having given notice a year ago, according to our Constitution. for a change of Part II, Article 7 of the Constitution of Synod, therefore,

Resolved, That, the following be added to said Article: " But if he comes from an approved Synod of the Evangelical Lutheran Church in the United States, with proper credentials, he may be received without examination."

Then the proposed changes in the name of the Evangelical Lutheran General Synod in North America, and the changes in Constitution of General Synod, as recommended on page 10, Arts. 2 and 3, printed Minutes of General Synod, of the year 1874, were adopted.

Item 5 of Committee on Letters and Petitions was again presented and adopted.

The Committee on Minutes of last Synod, read the following report which was received, and considered by items :

REPORT OF COMMITTEE ON MINUTES OF LAST MEETING OF SYNOD.

Your Committee beg leave to report the following:

1. On page 32 we find a resolution requiring all Ministers to furnish the Secretary the dates of their ordination, that he may make out the clerical roll according to such dates. Has this been done ?

2. On page 35 we find pledges made for the beneficiaries of Newberry College. Have these pledges been redeemed ?

3. On page 38 we find a resolution providing for the publication of the names of the persons, and amounts contributed to the Bachman Endowment to be published in the *Visitor* until all shall have been published. Has this this been done ?

4. On page 39 we find a resolution authorizing the Secretary to make arrangement previous to his coming to Synod for the publication of the Minutes of Synod. Has this duty been performed ?

5. On page 42 we find a resolution authorizing the Secretary to have one thousand blank certificates of attendance upon Synod struck off. Has this been done ?

6. On page 44 we find a resolution authorizing the Treasurer of Seminary Fund to pay to Rev. Prof. S. A. Repass, Five Hundred Dollars as the appropriation of this Synod to his salary. Has this been done ? •

On pages 31 and 32, we find the following questions negatively answered:

Item 7th. Did the Treasurer of Synodical Fund pay the Treasurer of the Missionary Fund, the balance of Fourteen Dollars due the latter. Has this been done ?

Item 8th. Have the delinquents paid their assessment to the Treasurer of Synod.

Respectfully submitted,

> J. D. BOWLES,
> A. W. LINDLER, } *Committee.*
> U. B. WHITES.

Item I. In part.

Item II. In part.

Item III. All but seven dollars.

Item IV. No.

Item V. Yes.

Item VI. Yes.

Item VII. Yes.

Item VIII. In part.

The report was adopted as a whole.

Mr. B. Rawl was excused from further attendance upon the sessions of Synod.

Synod adjourned to meet at 9 o'clock, A. M., October 13, 1876. Benediction by Rev. J. Hawkins.

FOURTH SESSION.

FRIDAY, Oct. 13th, 9 o'clock, A. M.

Synod met and was opened with prayer by Rev. Z. W. Bedenbaugh. The Secretary called the roll, and the minutes of yesterday were read and adopted.

Rev. Z. W. Bedenbaugh, Col. O. L. Schumpert, and Mr. G. T. Berg were excused from further attendance on the meeting of Synod after this morning's session.

The Committee on Conferences reported as follows :

Your Committee on Conferences would beg leave to report. The documents placed in their hands were :

1. The Minutes of Newberry Conference for the past Synodical year. In examining these minutes, we find evidence of active energetic work in the Master's cause. The reading of essays, and the discussion of important subjects, exert a wholesome influence upon Ministers and Laymen. This Body is no doubt developing the Church in liberality, and elevating the standard of piety among the members of the Church composing it. We found nothing in the Minutes calling the attention of this Synod.

2. A memorial from the Orangeburg Conference asking Synod to "define and declare the duties and powers of Conferences."

As the "duties and powers" of Conferences are manifold, your Committee can suggest no better *Rule* than that each Conference can attend to any duty, and exercise any power, not in violation of the word of God; nor in conflict with the duties of Church Councils, as shown in Ch IV of the Formula for the government and discipline of the Lutheran Church; nor in conflict with the duties and powers of Synod, as delineated in her organic law, the Constitution and By-Laws of Synod; nor in violation of its own Constitution.　　　　Respectfully submitted.

J. P. SMELTZER,
D. SHEALY,
A. D. L. MOSER.

Received and considered by items.

First item. Adopted.

Second item. Adopted, and as a whole.

———

Report of Committee on Treasurer of Widow's Fund was as follows :

REPORT OF COMMITTEE ON TREASURER OF WIDOW'S FUND.

LEXINGTON COURT HOUSE, S. C., 13th Oct., 1876.

To the President, Officers and Members of the " Evangelical Lutheran Synod of South Carolina, and Adjacent States :"

The undersigned Committee to whom was referred the report of the Treasurer of the "Widow's Fund," beg leave to say :

That the said Treasurer has handed in no report at this Session of Synod, owing to the fact that he has neither money nor assets on hand.

Respectfully submitted,

O. L. SCHUMPERT, } *Committee.*
J. D. SHEALY.

Adopted.

The Report of Committee on Treasurer of Endowment Fund was made and adopted :

The Committee to whom was referred the account of the Treasurer of the College Endowment Fund, ask leave to report, that they have carefully examined the same and find it correct, the proper entries being made in his book for monies received and receipts taken for amounts paid out by him. He has also given a full and correct statement of the pledges received by him in 1875, and paid over to the Treasurer of Newberry College. Our worthy Treasurer has, however, failed to comply with the resolution passed at the last session of this Body, in relation to assets in the hands of the Treasurers of the several funds belonging to the Synod. But although this omission has been made, we believe that the assets have been faithfully and correctly reported.

Respectfully submitted,

GERHARD MULLER,
P. E. WISE,
A. H. WHEELER.

O. L. SCHUMPERT, IN ACCT. WITH J. P. SMELTZER, D. D.

(RECEIPTS.)

1875.

15–20 Oct.—Rev. W. S. Bowman's charge Profs. salary			$	75 00
" Capt. G. S. Hacker, self,	"	"		30 00
" Rev. P. Derrick, self,	"	"		10 00
" Corinth Church,	"	"		10 00
" St. Mark's Church,	"	"		20 00
" St. Michael, No. 9,	"	"		12 50
" Rev. J. H. Bailey, self,	"	"		15 00
" Rev. T. W. Dosh's charge St. Johns, Prof. salary.				100 00
" B. Kreps, No. 1,	"	"		25 00
" O. L. Schumpert, self,	"	"		50 00
" J. K. Schumpert, "	"	"		25 00
" Rev. H. W. Kuhns, charge Luther Chapel...				35 00
" Rev. J. D. Bolles, charge No. 12				50 00
" Rev. D. Kyser charge No. 5				10 00
" Rev. S. S. Rahn, charge No. 10				20 00
" Rev. J. A. Sligh, (St. Paul and Macedonia)..				75 00
" Rev. J. H. W. Werts, Trinity Church				35 00
" Rev. S. T. Hallman's charge				50 00
" S. F. Felder, self				5 00
" Rev. H. S. Wingard, Prosperity				50 00
" Rev. A. W. Lindler, St. John				5 00
" Rev. Samuel Bouknight's charge				7 50
Total			$715	00

1875.
18 Oct.—Paid Rev. J. P. Smeltzer............$652 50
19   "   " 62 50
                                        ——————— $715 00
The vouchers are herewith annexed.   •
Respectfully submitted,
O. L. SCHUMPERT,
B. E. T. N. C.
Lexington, S. C., Oct. 11, 1876.

———

O. L. SCHUMPERT, IN ACCOUNT WITH THE BACHMAN
ENDOWMENT FUND, NEWBERRY COLLEGE, S. C.

To amount received at and since last meeting of Synod...$ 70 96
To amount reported on hand at Synod of 1875.......... 840 38
                                                      ————
Total on hand 10th Oct., 1876....................$911 34
The envelopes and other vouchers in relation to said fund, are
herewith submitted and made a part of this report.
Respectfully submitted,
O. L. SCHUMPERT, *B. E. T. Newberry College.*
Lexington, S. C., Oct. 11, 1876.

One-third interest in 300 acres land in Newberry........$800 00
One Personal Bond of $100 00 at 10 per cent........... 100 00
The Peoples' Saving Institution, Charleston, S. C........ 10 00
                                                        ————
Cash on hand................................$910 00
Respectfully submitted,
O. L. SCHUMPERT, *B. E. T. of Newberry College.*
Lexington, S. C., Oct. 11, 1876.

The Committee on the report of Treasurer of Synod was presented and adopted:

P. E. WISE, IN ACCOUNT WITH THE SYNOD OF SOUTH CAROLINA.

1875.   Dr.

Oct. 15	—	Received Congregational Contributions for Synod at St. Luke's Church	$387	44
"	"	Rev. D. Kyser, for Beneficiaries	5	00
"	"	A. J. Younginger, for Beneficiaries	1	00
"	"	, Rev. E. Caughman, for Beneficiaries	6	00
"	"	Miss Vida Day Bedenbaugh, for Beneficiaries	1	00
"	"	R. T. C. Hunter, for Beneficiaries	5	00
"	"	Jacob Setzler, for Beneficiaries	1	00
"	"	Rev. Z. W. Bedenbaugh, for Beneficiaries	5	00
"	"	P. E. Wise, for Beneficiaries	5	00
Nov. 4	"	J. F. Schirmer, for Beneficiaries	5	00
"	"	F. H. Honour, for Beneficiaries	5	00
"	"	Rev. J. H. Honour, for Beneficiaries	10	00
"	"	Rev. Dr. Dosh, for advertising	76	00
Dec. 28	"	Rev. J. D. Shirey, for Beneficiaries	15	00
"	"	A. Berly, for Beneficiaries	5	00
"	"	Rev. H. W. Kuhns, for Beneficiaries	10	00
"	"	O. L. Schumpert, for Beneficiaries	5	00
1876.				
Jan. 28	—	Received, Rev. W. S. Bowman, D. D., for Beneficiaries	25	00
Feb.	"	Bethlehem charge, for Beneficiaries	15	00
"	"	Faculty of N. College, Beneficiaries	10	00
March 4	"	Rev. E. A. Wingard, for Beneficiaries	5	00
" 6	"	O. L. Schumpert on (W. S. B. note)	80	00
" 15	"	Rev. H. S. Wingard	10	00
April 22	"	Mrs. Fred Muller, for Beneficiaries	5	00
May 15	"	T. W. Holloway, for Beneficiaries	5	00
" 22	"	O. L. Schumpert on (W. S. B. note)	19	45
Oct. 6	"	Rev. J. F. Probst, for Beneficiaries	5	00
"	"	Rev. Edwin A. Bolles, Beneficiaries	5	00
"	"	Rev. J. A. Sligh, for Beneficiaries	10	00
"	"	Rev. J. D. Bowles, for Beneficiaries	5	00
"	"	Rev. J. B. Haskell, for Beneficiaries	5	00
"	"	Rev. S. T. Hallman, for Beneficiaries	10	00

$761 89

1875.		CR.	
Oct. 15—Balance due Treasurer	$	7	26
" 18—Paid Rev. S. T. Hallman, per order of Synod..		16	40
" 21—Paid L. E. Busby, Beneficiary for 1875		73	25
" 21—Paid Wm. Stoudemeyer, Beneficiary for 1875..		73	25
" 21—Paid J. W. S. Sheppard, Beneficiary for 1875...		20	00
Nov. 24—Paid for printing minutes of Synod		156	50
" 24—Paid for express on money			50
Dec. 8—Paid Wm. Stoudemeyer, Beneficiary		43	00
" 8—Paid registered letter			13
" 29—Paid J. P. Smeltzer,D.D., for Werts and Sheppard Beneficiaries....		35	00
1876.			
Feby.—Paid Werts and Sheppard, Beneficiaries		58	28
March 7—Paid Wm. Stoudemeyer, Beneficiary		80	00
" 15—Paid J. D. Werts, Beneficiary		10	00
April 27—Paid J. D. Werts, Beneficiary		5	00
May 15—Paid J. D. Werts, Beneficiary		10	00
" 25—Paid Wm. Studemeyer, beneficiaries		29	45
" 25—Paid registered letter			13
June 29—Paid J. P. Smeltzer for W. Stoudemeyer		4	00
Oct. 6—Paid J. P. Smeltzer for W. Stoudemeyer		18	55
" 6—Paid J. P. Smeltzer for Werts and Sheppard....		106	45

$747 15

Balance in hands of Treasurer............... 14 74

$761 89

We, the Committee appointed to audit the account of Treasurer of Synod, have carefully examined the same and find the entries correctly made, and properly vouched for.

Respectfully submitted,
U. B. WHITES,
T. J. BOOZER, } *Committee.*
J. L. RAST,

The Committee on the state of religion, made the following report :

REPORT OF THE STATE OF RELIGION.

By a careful review of the Reports of the Pastors on the state of religion, we have arrived at the following conclusions :

1. That faithfulness and zeal on the part of the Ministers, in preaching the word, in making pastoral visits, and in catechizing the young, is clearly evident, and that these labors have been performed and great self-denial most cheerfully, in order that the glory of God might be promoted, and the Kingdom of Christ extended.

5

2. It is also evident that the attendance upon public worship, and the participation in the other ministrations of the sanctuary, on the part of our people, have been quite commendable. As a consequence of all this, most of the Churches have been greatly revived, the zeal of the people in the cause of Christ has been increased, and the spiritual condition of the membership improved.

3. One of the most hopeful features about the statements before us, is the special attention that has been paid to the Sabbath School cause, the formation of interesting Bible classes, and the untiring efforts made to gather the young into the fold of the Redeemer. After all, the young are the chief hope of the Church.

4. It should be a source of gratification to the members and Ministers of the Church to know, Newberry College still lives, and still claims the prayers and patronage of our people. Many of the sons of the Church are resorting thither to receive that preparatory training which will fit them for efficient service in the Lord's vineyard.

5. We also refer with great pleasure to the increased spirit and interest that has been awakened among our Ministers and people on the important subject of Missions, especially *Home Missions*. Many of the waste places of Zion are being looked after, congregations organized, and the bread of life broken to the poor and neglected.

Without attempting to enumerate minutely all the signs of improvement, and whilst we are laboring amidst many difficulties and discouragements, there is great cause for rejoicing that there is a gradual and steady church growth among us from year to year. New church edifices and parsonages are erected, the spirit of liberality in the support of the benevolent operations of the Church has been greatly increased, and our future is hopeful and encouraging. Our prayer is that the kind fraternal spirit now existing among our Ministers may continue, and that the blessing of God may rest upon us and upon all our labors.

Respectfully submitted,

J. F. PROBST,
J. A. SLIGH,
D. G. WAYNE.

Adopted.

The Committee on Boundary Line of Conferences made their report which was adopted:

REPORT OF COMMITTEE ON CONFERENCE BOUNDARY.

Your Committee on a Boundary Line between the Newberry and Edgefield Conferences, recommend that the line as now existing be changed, and that the line be from Broad River by Bethlehem to the Aiken road below Prosperity, thence to Leesville on South, thus throwing Bethlehem, St. Paul's and St. Michael's charges into the lower division, and all the Churches North and West of that line, into the upper division.

J. HAWKINS,
J. II. BAILEY,
J. W. DREHER.

The Committee on report of Delegates to General Synod, reported the following:

REPORT OF THE DELEGATES TO GENERAL SYNOD.

Of your delegation to the tenth Convention of the Evangelical Lutheran General Synod in North America, only three were in attendance, two Ministers, and one Layman.

The meeting was harmonious, and much business of importance to our Southern Church was transacted.

Every department of our Church work, as presented before the General Synod, gave evidence of healthful and progressive developement. In the special work of Missions but little has been done, as compared with the great work before us. The regret is that we have so few men, and so little means, with which to prosecute the work with that earnestness and vigor which it demands.

With regard to the *Lutheran Visitor* you have been informed. It might be well to state here that Rev. T. W. Dosh, D. D., was continued editor, though no longer a member of General Synod, because of the general satisfaction he had given by his able management of the paper. and also to prevent any confusion or temporary stoppage that might occur from an entire change of hands. We are glad to state that up to the meeting of General Synod, its expenditures were exceeded by its receipts, though not by any amount that might be considered a remuneration to the editors for their arduous labors. Vide Res. I and II.

The Theological Seminary we are glad to report as in a prosperous condition. The President in his report has referred you to the duty devolving on this Body to nominate the Professor which she will sustain, and it will be only necessary for us to refer to the grounds for such a step.

a. As was shown at the General Synod, the funds in the hands of those engaged in raising an endowment fund for the Seminary, would command such an income, that the other Synods composing the General Synod, could by contributing the same amounts they have been heretofore paying, sustain another professor.

b. The session beginning in September 1877, will open with three classes which will demand more labor than one Professor can perform.

c. A three years course with one Professor can be only nominal, and hence the Seminary will lose her respect and character, and would soon become but a feeder for other Seminaries better endowed and maned.

To meet the emergency arising by the session of 1877 beginning before the next meeting of our Synod, we must nominate at this session. The matter of securing another Professor was left in the hands of the officers of the Board of Directors who are to act as the circumstances justify and demand.

At our request it was declared that this Synod nominate the incumbent of the "first chair," viz: That of Systematic and Practical Theology.

The following reasons led to this request: (*a*) To vote intelligently we should know in what department the Professor would give instruction. (*b*) As the Synod longest interested in the Seminary, and indeed its founder, we felt it was not seeking too much to ask for the South Carolina Synod, the right to remain first in the choice and support of a Professor. (*c*) We thought that by supporting this chair, we kept up better the historic connection of the Seminary of the General Synod, with the Seminary of the South Carolina Synod. Vide III, IV, V.

Action was taken in several instances looking to the closer union of all Lutherans in the United States; as for instance, the sending of Delegates to other General Bodies; the effort to be made to have one Book of Worship for the use of the whole Lutheran Church; and of especial interest to us, the effort to unite all the Synods South in one General Body.

We also call attention to the amounts for which this Body has been assessed :

1. For incidental expenses of the Theological Seminary *this* Synod is assessed $38, (see page 11, Minutes of General Synod.)

2. The amount to be paid by this Synod for the printing of the Minutes as will be made known by the Treasurer of General Synod. We would also call attention to the amount expended by your delegates in attending the last Convention of Synod. Vide Res. VII.

The next session of General Synod will be held D. V. in Newberry South Carolina, on Thursday before the first Lord's Day in May, 1878.

Respectfully submitted,

H. S. WINGARD.

1. *Resolved*, That although the chief editor of the *Lutheran Visitor* is no longer under the jurisdiction of our General Synod, yet we most heartily endorse and commend his continuance in that office.

2. *Resolved*, Every member of this Body make renewed and special efforts during the present Synodical year to extend the circulation of the paper.

3. *Resolved*, That appreciating the reasons stated in this report, and having learned that the other Synods in our General Synod will undertake the support of a second Professor in September, 1877, we now proceed to nominate a Professor to the Chair of Systematic and Practical Theology.

4. *Resolved*, That until the Professor now nominated shall be confirmed by the Seminary Board, and a second Professor actually employed in the Seminary, the present financial arrangement between this Synod and our General Synod shall continue.

5. *Resolved*, That the names of persons suitable for this high and responsible position be presented to Synod, and after due discussion the nomination be made by ballot.

6. *Resolved*, That the legislation of our General Synod, looking to a more complete organic unity and administrative uniformity in the Lutheran Church in this country, meet with our hearty approval.

7. *Resolved*, That the incidental expenses of the Theological Seminary amounting to $38, and our *pro rata* amount for the printing of the Minutes of the General Synod, and the expenses of your Delegates be paid.

Respectfully submitted,

J. P. SMELTZER,
W. S. BOWMAN,
J. HAWKINS.

Received and adopted by items.

Item I. Adopted.
Item II. Adopted.
Item III. Adopted.
Item IV. Adopted.
Item V. Adopted.
Item VI. Adopted.
Item VII. Adopted.

The report was then adopted as a whole.

Resolved, That the Treasurer of the Seminary Fund be requested to pay the *pro rata* amount fixed by the General Synod, ($38) being their portion to meet the incidental expenses of the Seminary (see resolution of General Synod, page 11.)

Whereas, The General Synod passed a resolution, (see page 34) that the Treasurer of the General Synod be requested to make a *pro rata* assessment in each District Synod, to pay for the printing of the Minutes, and in accordance with the resolution it has been made, and the portion for our Synod is $34. The Treasurer would therefore request an order for the payment of the same.

Resolved, That the Treasurer of the Seminary Fund be ordered to pay the same from funds in his hands.

Rev. W. S. Bowman, D. D., Corresponding Delegate to Virginia

Synod, made the following report, which was received and adopted:

REPORT OF DELEGATE TO SYNOD OF VIRGINIA.

It was the privilege of the undersigned to attend the last Convention of the Evangelical Lutheran Synod of Virginia, which held its Sessions at Strasburg, Virginia, commencing August 3d, 1876.

Your Delegate was most cordially received, and the deepest interest was manifested in our work and in our welfare.

Among the liberal and enlightened efforts of this body, is a prudent tendency to unite all the Lutheran bodies in the South, in sympathy, in effort, and in organic union.

A Delegate was appointed to this body.   W. S. BOWMAN.

A letter was read from Rev. J. I. Miller, Corresponding Delegate from the Virginia Synod, when it was

Resolved, That we regret the inability of the Delegate from the Synod of Virginia to attend this meeting of the South Carolina Synod, and heartily reciprocate the fraternal expressions contained in his letter.

Rev. G. A. Hough was excused from further attendance upon the Sessions of Synod.

Synod adjourned for divine service.

Benediction by Rev. D. Kyser.

The sermon on education was preached at 11 o'clock, by Rev. H. W. Kuhns from 2 Tim. ii: 2. After which a liberal collection was taken up for beneficiary education.

AFTERNOON SESSION.

3 o'clock, P. M.

Synod re-assembled and was opened with prayer by Rev. B. Kreps.

It was

Resolved, That the Treasurer of Synod be directed to pay the bill of Walker, Evans & Cogswell for printing certificates of Ordination and Parochial Reports.

The expenses of the Investigating Committee appointed by Newberry Conference, amounting to $20 10, were ordered to be paid.

Resolved, That this Synod respectfully, but earnestly requests all our Pastors to preach a Centennial sermon on the Sunday nearest the 31st October, (Reformation Day) or as soon thereafter as possible; presenting not only the history of the respective congregations, but making also proper reference to the direct influence of the great Reformation upon the Church, and in the development of civil government throughout the world.

Resolved, That, hereafter any Minister accepting of a charge within our bounds, shall not, under penalty of being censured by Synod, enter upon his labors until the charge shall have made a satisfactory settlement with their former Pastor, and that this shall be considered the standing rule among us, and printed on the face of our Minutes from year to year.

Resolved, That Rev. J. H. Bailey's expenses to Georgia Synod be paid.

Resolved, That the Treasurer of Synod be ordered to pay the expenses of Delegates to General Synod.

The business of the afternoon was taken up, which was in reference to item second in the Report of the Committee on the Report of the Board of Trustees of Newberry College.

Pending the item, Synod adjourned to meet in Ministerium.

Prayer by Rev. J. H. Honour.

Sermon at night by Mr. S. P. Hughes, from Luke, ii: 10.

FIFTH SESSION.

SATURDAY, OCTOBER 14, 1876, 9 O'CLOCK, A. M.

Synod convened, and was opened with prayer by Rev. J. H. Probst.

The Secretary called the roll, and the minutes were read and approved.

A letter was read from Rev. C. F. Bansemer, asking to be excused from the Sessions of this Synod.

He was excused.

Then the business of the hour was taken up, being item second in the Report of the Committee on the Report of the Board of Trustees of Newberry College. After mature discussion, the Report was adopted.

The Committee appointed to nominate a Committee of five to receive bids for the location of Newberry College, reported the names of Revs. J. Hawkins, J. A. Sligh, H. S. Wingard, Col. O. L. Schumpert, and Mr. T. W. Holloway, who were unanimously elected.

An election was entered into for a Professor to fill the Chair of Systematic and Practical Theology in the Theological Seminary, which resulted in the unanimous election of Rev. S. A. Repass, D. D.

Revs. J. A. Sligh and A. D. L. Moser were excused from further attendance upon the sessions of Synod.

Synod adjourned for Divine Service.

Benediction by the President.

At 11 o'clock the Missionary sermon was preached by Rev. J. D. Bowles, from Mark XVI,, 15.

The following members of the Missionary Society were received:

ANNUAL MEMBERS OF THE MISSIONARY SOCIETY.

Rev. D. Shealy	$ 1 00	Mrs. D. L. Boozer	$ 1 00
" J. N. Derrick	1 00	Mrs. Mary L. Hawkins	1 00
" B. Kreps	1 00	Mrs. M. E. Dreher	1 00
" D. Kyser	1 00	Mrs. J. J. Taylor	1 00
" W. S. Bowman, D.D.	1 00	Miss M. L. Barre	1 00
" J. P. Smeltzer, D. D.	1 00	Mr. A. Roberts	1 00
" C. P. Boozer	1 00	Mr. E J. George	1 00
" E. Caughman	2 00	Mr. J. S. Roberts	1 00
Mr. P. H. Caughman	1 00	Mr. J. Hiller	1 00
Mr. B. Rawl	1 00	Misses A. V.&C.E.Meetze	1 00
Mr. W. W. Barre	1 00	Mr. U. B. Whites	1 00
Mr. J. N. Barre	1 00	Mrs. U. B. Whites	1 00
Mr. W. H. Dickert	1 00	Miss Corrie McFall	1 00
Mr. W. J. Asman	1 00	Mrs. M. M. Kibler	1 00
Miss Lou Asman	1 00	Mrs. N. A. Wheeler	1 00
Mr. B. L. Dreher	1 00	Mr. J. M. Wheeler	1 00
Mrs. B. L. Dreher	1 00	Mr. A. M. Wise	1 00
Dr. L. Bachman Folk	1 00	Miss Mollie Bobb	1 00
Miss Alice Nunamaker	1 00	Maj. P. E. Wise	1 00
Rev. J. D. Bowles	1 00	Mrs. H. S. Wingard	1 00
Rev. J. H. Werts	1 00	Mrs. A. H. Wheeler	1 00
Rev. J. H. Bailey	1 00	Mr. J. W. Bowers	1 00
Mr. A. C. Moyer	1 00	Mr. H. S. Boozer	1 00
Mr. T. J. Boozer	1 00	Mrs. M. E. Stoudemeyer.	1 00
Mrs. Ann Caughman	1 00	Miss Ella Seas	1 00
Rev. A. D. L. Moser	1 00	Rev. Edwin A. Bolles	1 00
Dr. G. Muller	1 00	Rev. J. A. Sligh	1 00
Mr. T. W. Halloway	1 00	Rev. B. F. Berry	1 00
Mrs. A. O. Holloway	1 00	Mrs. J. A. Sligh	1 00
Mrs. R. H. Bernhard	1 00	Mrs. M. C. Rawl	1 00
Mr. C. Erhardt	1 00	Mrs. A. C. Turnipseed	1 00
Rev. H. W. Kuhns	1 00	Mrs. Lou Souter	1 00
Mrs. M. E. Wilson	1 00	Mr. J. E. Chapman	1 00
Mrs. S. E. Caughman	1 00	Miss Annie Rouch	1 00
Mrs. Elizabeth Barre	1 00	Mr. Wm. J. Asman	2 00

```
          Total Annual Members....................$ 72 00
            "    Amount for Home Missions.............. 164 95
            "        "       Foreign Missions............. 36 05
            "        "       Sunday collections............. 25 11
                                                        ─────────
                                                        $298 11
```

U. B. WHITES, *Treasurer.*

CONGREGATIONAL CONTRIBUTIONS TO THE MIS-SIONARY FUND. (HOME MISSION.)

Rev. H. W. Kuhns's charge	$ 5	00
" J. D. Bowles's charge	10	00
" S. T. Hallman's charge	13	00
" J. A. Sligh's charge	15	00
" J. H. W.Werts's charge	19	05
" C. P. Boozer's Missionary Society, St. Mark's	13	75
" D. Kizer's charge	7	95
" S. Bouknight's charge	8	55
" Z. W. Bedenbaugh's charge	5	00
" W. S. Bowman,'s D. D. charge	12	55
" E. Caughman's charge	5	00
" J. Hawkins's, St. Michael	25	00
Graniteville Church	2	50
Rev. J. D. Shirey's, St. Matthew's	10	20
" " Beth Eden	8	20
" " Liberty Hill	4	20
Total	$164	95

CONTRIBUTIONS FOR FOREIGN MISSIONS.

Rev. J. F. Probst's charge	$ 2	00
" J. D. Shirey's, St. Matthew's	9	40
" " Beth Eden	6	50
" " Liberty Hill		90
" H. S. Wingard, Sunday School	6	25
" J. D. Bowles's charge	8	00
" J. H. W. Werts, Sunday School	3	00
Jacob F. Schirmer	1	00
Miss Mary L. Schirmer	1	00
" E. C. Tovey	1	00
" E. A. Boinest		50
J. Bachman Boinest		50
W. Bowman Boinest		50
Mrs. K. Boinest		50
" May Rikard		50
Total	$ 41	55

AFTERNOON SESSION.

3 o'clock, P. M.

Synod re-assembled in the interest of the Missionary Society, and was opened with prayer by Rev. J. D. Shirey.

6

Rev. E. Caughman then made a report concerning the Graniteville Mission, which was received as information.

Rev. J. B. Haskell was excused from further attendance upon the sessions of Synod.

Committee on the Report of the Treasurer of the Missionary Society, made the following report:

U. B. WHITES, TREASURER OF MISSIONARY SOCIETY, IN ACCT. WITH THE SOUTH CAROLINA SYNOD.

1875.	DR.	CR.
Oct. 15—To balance on hand................. 129 46		
" 16— " amount received at Synod........ 357 71		
Dec. 18—By cash paid Rev. J. F. Probst.......		75 00
" " " Express..............		50
1876.		
May 2—By cash paid Rev. J. F. Probst........		75 00
" " " Express................		75
Aug. 1— " " Rev. J. F. Probst........		75 00
" " " Express		• 75
Oct. 7— " " Rev. J. F. Probst.......		75 00
" " " Express................		50
" 9—To cash received from Rev. J. F. Probst for sundry collections.............. 15 00		
By Balance.......................		199 67

$502 17—$502 17

U. B. WHITES, *Treasurer.*

The Committee to whom was referred the account of the Treasurer of the Missionary Society, would respectfully report that they have examined the same and found correct. Vouchers were presented for payments made, and the report leaves a balance in his hands of one hundred and ninety-nine dollars and sixty-seven cents.

Respectfully submitted,

JACOB F. SCHIRMER.
E. CROUT,
B. RAWLS.

Rev. J. F. Probst, Superintendant of Missions, read the following report:

MISSIONARY'S REPORT.

To the Synod of South Carolina:

DEAR BRETHREN :—By the help of the Lord I have performed the labors of another year, and I take pleasure in making a brief statement of my operations:

1. In Abbeville I have visited the little German congregation in Abbeville County during the year. Amidst many discouragements which mostly arise from their indigent condition, they have still been very faithful in their attendance on the ordinances of religion. Some walk from eight to ten miles to Church. They always seem glad to see me come among them, and in many ways show their appreciation of my services. Several families left, but others have come in from Canada, and from Pennsylvania, so that we have more there now than at first. My next appointment among them is on the 4th Sunday of this month.

2. Newberry. I have also visited the little German flock in Newberry County, frequently during the year. Here the number is not so large as at the other places, but it is an interesting little company. I had a very pleasant Communion season with them on the 4th Sunday of September. One person was confirmed.

3. Anderson. I have also a number of times visited and conducted religious services with the Germans of Anderson and vicinity. On the 26th of August last, I succeeded in organizing them, and held the communion with them. They are the most interesting emigrants I have met with in the State, and thus far I have enjoyed my visits among them very much. Hon. B. F. Crayton and other American gentlemen take a deep interest in them, and assist me in my labors among them. I promised to meet them again on the 4th Sunday in November.

The collections this year amounted to $15.

Respectfully,

J. F. PROBST.

When it was,

Resolved, That Rev. J. F. Probst be continued as Superintendant of Missions at the salary of $300 per annum.

Resolved, That Rev. J. F. Probst be appointed to preach the Missionary sermon at the next meeting of this Synod, and Rev. J. D. Shirey be his alternate.

On motion the Executive Committee was continued, viz : Rev. H. W. Kuhns, J. A. Sligh, H. S. Wingard, and Messrs. W. W. Houseal, O. L. Schumpert, U. B. Whites, and H. S. Boozer.

Synodical business was resumed.

Resolved, That Revs. H. W. Kuhns, J. A. Sligh, and Col. O. L. Schumpert, be appointed a Committee to confer with the Agent of the Endowment Fund.

It was then,

Resolved, That the Committee of the Board of Trustees be authorized to make arrangements as to the character of the Bonds to be given in raising the Endowment Fund of Newberry College.

Resolved, That the Treasury of Widow's Fund be abolished.

Resolved, That the Foreign Missionary money in hands of the Treasurer be forwarded to Mr. Martin Buehler, Philadelphia, Treasurer of the Foreign Missionary Fund.

On motion it was,

Resolved, That Rev. H. W. Kuhns be requested to furnish a copy of his sermon on Education, preached at the present meeting of Synod, to *Lutheran Visitor* for publication.

Resolved, That hereafter this Body requests that the Pastor *loci,* in which the sessions of Synod will take place, do make timely arrangements with the Railroads for the reduction of the travelling expenses of the members of Synod.

It was moved and adopted that the Treasurer of the Endowment Fund be authorized to pay the interest of monies now in his hands to the Faculty of Newberry College.

On motion the following was adopted:

Resolved, That when this Synod adjourn, it adjourns to meet on Tuesday before the third Lord's day in Oct., 1877, and that St. Matthew's Lutheran Church, Orangeburg County, S. C., be the place of meeting.

It was,

Resolved, That the thanks of this Synod are due to the members of St. Stephen's Church, and all others who have so kindly entertained the members of Synod during its Sessions, in their midst.

Resolved, That the President read this resolution from the pulpit, to-morrow after divine service.

Resolved, That the Secretary have one thousand copies of the Minutes of the present session of Synod printed and distributed in the usual order.

The Committee on appropriations read their report, which was received and adopted.

REPORT OF COMMITTEE ON APPROPRIATIONS.

Your Committee respectfully submit, that the applications of five young men for aid, have been presented to them.

We find in the hands of the Treasurer of Synod and Education, only about $350 of available funds. To meet the demands of these young men, we ought to have eight hundred dollars. In view of the depleted condition of our treasury, we recommend that the amount on hand be equally divided between the five applicants for aid, and that pledges and contributions be called for to meet the deficiency.

Respectfully submitted,

J. D. SHIREY,
J. P. SMELTZER,
U. B. WHITES.

When the following pledges were called for and made:

Pastorate No. 9....................................$10 00
Bethlehem Charge................................... 10 00
Pastorate No. 12................................... 10 00
St. Stephen's Church............................... 10 00
Rev. B. Kreps's Charge............................. 10 00
Rev. H. S. Wingard's Charge........................ 10 00
Rev. J. B. Haskell's charge........................ 10 00
Wentworth Street Lutheran Church................... 20 00
St. John's Church, Charleston...................... 10 00
Rev. S. T. Hallman's Charge........................ 10 00
Rev. C. P. Boozer's Charge......................... 10 00
Rev. J. A. Sligh................................... 30 00

on Rev. M. Whittle's account.

Upon the nomination by the Committee consisting of Revs. J. H. Honour, B. Kreps, J. H. W. Werts, the following Board of Trustees of Newberry College, were elected:

Rev. H. W. Kuhns, Rev. J. A. Sligh, Rev. J. Hawkins, Thos. W. Holloway, Esq., Dr. A. E. Norman, Hon. D. Bieman, Maj. P. E. Wise, Mr. W. Haltiwanger, Maj. G. Leaphart, Rev. H. S. Wingard, O. L. Schumpert, Esq., Mr. H. S. Boozer, Rev. J. D. Shirey, Rev. S. T. Hallman, Col. J. J. Norton, Mr. C. Ehrhardt, Rev. W. S. Bowman, D. D., Maj. Henry A. Metts.

The report of special Committee on report of Corresponding Secretary, was made:

The Special Committee appointed to consider that portion of the Corresponding Secrtary's Report, which refers to his correspondence with Rev. M. Whittle, beg leave to report as follows:

The spirit and tenor of Mr. Whittle's correspondence, indicates an unmistakable disposition not to meet his obligations in this matter unless legally compelled to do so, but we recommend the continued efforts of the Corresponding Secretary, to secure his dues.   Respectfully submitted,

W. S. BOWMAN,
J. H. HONOUR,
G. T. BERG.

Adopted.

The following Delegates were elected to Sister Synods:

Rev. J. Hawkins, Corresponding Delegate to the Georgia Synod, and Rev. J. H. Bailey, Alternate.

Rev. W. S. Bowman, D. D.. Corresponding Delegate to the North Carolina Synod, and Rev. J. F. Probst, Alternate.

Synod adjourned to meet in Ministerium.

Benediction by the President.

Sermon at night by Rev. J. P. Smeltzer, D. D., from St. Luke XVIII; 26.

CONGREGATIONAL CONTRIBUTIONS RECEIVED AT SYNOD AT ST. STEPHEN'S CHURCH.

LEXINGTON COUNTY, S. C., Oct. 10. 1876.

Received of Rev. H. W. Kuhns's Charge,
Synodical Fund................... 35 00
Beneficiary Education............. 35 00
——— $70 00

Received of Rev. J. Hawkins's Charge,
St. Micheal's Church Synodical Fund 25 00
Bethel " " " 17 00
Mt. Olivet " " " 16 00
St. Andrew's " " " 10 00
——— $68 00

Received of Rev. J. F. Probst's Charge,
St. John's Walhalla Synodical Fund.. 5 00
Beneficiary Education.............. 7 35
——— $12 35

Received of Rev. J. D. Bolles's Charge,
Synodical Fund................... 10 00
Beneficiary Education............. 20 00
——— $30 00

Received of Rev. H. S. Wingard's Charge,
Newville Church, Synodical Fund.......... $14 25

Received of J. H. W. Werts's Charge,
Pine Grove Church, Synodical Fund 20 00
Trinity " " " 22 10
——— $42 10

Received of Rev. S. T. Hallman's Charge.
Synodical Fund................... 13 00
Beneficiary Education............. 13 00
——— $26 00

Received of Rev. Z. W. Bedenbaugh's Church,
Synodical Fund................... 5 00
Beneficiary Education............. 10 00
——— $15 00

Received of Rev. G. A. Hough's Charge,
St. John's Church, Calk's Road Synodical Fund........................ $6 25

Received of Rev. J. D. Shirey's Charge,
Beth Eden Church, Synodical Fund.. 13 80
"   "   Ben'l Education.. 4 35
St. Mathews's "   Synodical Fund... 17 25
"   "   Ben'y Education.. 7 30
Liberty Hill "   Synodical Fund... 1 70
".   "   "   Ben'y Education.. 5 00
                                   ——— $59 40

Received of Rev. J. A. Sligh's Charge,
Synodical Fund.............. 5 00
Beneficiary Education............ 50 00
                                   ——— $55 00

Received of Rev. W. S. Bowman, D. D. Charge,
Wentworth Street Lutheran Church,
Synodical Fund 35 00

Received of Rev. C. P. Boozer's Charge,
Corinth Church, Synodical Fund..... 6 00
St. Mark's "   "   " 5 73
                                   ——— $11 73

Received of Rev. D. Shealy's Charge,
Synodical Fund......................... 10 60

Received of Rev. E. Caughman's Charge,
Good Hope Church, Synodical Fund........ 2 10

Received of Rev. J. H. Bailey's Charge,
Sandy Run Church, Synodical Fund.. 20 50
St. Stephen's "   "   " 36 79
"   " Beneficiary Education 12 95
Providence Church, Synodical Fund.. 4 15
                                   ——— $74 39

Received of Rev. D. Kyser's Charge, Synodical Fund....$10 45

Received of Rev. B. Kreps's Charge,
Mt. Pleasant Church, Synodical Fund 15 11
St. Nicholas   "   "   "   1 50
Bethlehem   "   "   "   1 25
                                   ——— $17 86

Received of Rev. S. Bouknight's Charge,
Synodical Fund......................... 2 45

Received of Rev. S. S. Rahn's Charge,
Synodical Fund......................... 12 55

Received of Wm. Haltiwanger, Beneficiary Education....$10 00
"   " Capt. D. G. Wayne   "   " 5 00
"   " W. A. Whittle, per Rev. J. A. Sligh........ 30 00

SUNDAY EXCERCISES.

At 10 o'clock A. M., Prayer Meeting.

At 11 o'clock, Services preparatory to the Lord's Supper, by
Rev. J. H. Honour, and the Ordination sermon preached by the
Rev. W. S. Bowman, D. D., from St. Mark, III; 14.

After which Mr. S. P. Hughes was solemnly ordained and set
apart to the holy office of the Christian Ministry, according to the
formula contained in the book of worship. This service was performed by Rev. Edwin A. Bolles, President; Rev. W. S. Bowman.
D. D., Vice President; Rev. C. P. Boozer, Secretary; Rev. J. P.
Smeltzer, D. D., Rev. J. H. Honour, and Rev. J. Hawkins.

At 11 o'clock, Rev. J. F. Probst preached in the M. E. Church
from John IX: 4.

At 11 o'clock Rev. J. D. Bowles preached in the A. M. E.
Church from Matt. VII: 21.

The Lord's Supper was administered to the members of Synod,
and a large number of the disciples of Christ.

After a recess, Synod met in the interests of the Sunday School.
An address was delivered by Rev. H. W. Kuhns.

SIXTH SESSION.

SUNDAY, Oct. 15, 4 o'CLOCK, P. M.

Synod met, and was opened with prayer by Rev. J. F. Probst.
The Minutes of the previous Session was read and approved,

Synod was then closed by the President, according to our established formula, to meet at the time and place before specified.

CORNELIUS P. BOOZER,

Recording Secretary of the Synod of So. Ca. and Adjacent States.

PAROCHIAL REPORT.

MINISTERS AND VACANT CHURCHES REPORTING	No. of Congregations	Children Baptized	Baptism	Confirmation	Certificate	Dismissions	Suspensions	Excommunications	Restorations	Communicants	Death of Members	Funerals	Prayer Meetings	Sunday Schools	Teachers	Scholars	Synodical Fund	Home Missions	Foreign Missions	Beneficiary Education	Endowment Fund	Local Objects	Salary Promised	Salary Due	No. of Pastorate
Rev. B. Kreps	3	16	3	4	1			3	1	188	2	8	1	2	8	45	$17 98	$13 00		$13 00		$21 66	$500 00	$360 00	1
Rev. S. T. Hallman	2	9		11					1	158	3	3		2	16	86	13 00	19 05	$3 00			1200 00	685 00	168 82	2
Rev. J. H. W. Wertz	2	8	3	14	2	2				177		3	1	2	10	100	42 00	7 10		12 75		130 00	500 00	181 00	3
Rev. J. H. Bailey	3	35	6	15		5		1		280	4	15	3	3	23	104	61 29	7 95				22 00	400 00	125 00	4
Rev. D. Kyser	3	29	8	21	3	5				296	4	8	3	4	12	140	10 45						127 00	88 00	5
Rev. D. Shealy	3	14		28		13		7		250	3		4	3	8	70	10 70	13 75		40 00		90 00	250 00		6
Rev. C. P. Boozer*	3	15	3	22		3				293		5	4	4	24	220	13 00	25 00				50 00	900 00	114 50	7
Rev. J. Hawkins*	4	12								340	1	3	2	5	30	230	68 00				5 00	100 00	580 00		—
Rev. S. S. Rahn	2	8		3	1					191		3	3	2	6	60		15 00	8 00	50 00			600 00	130 00	9
Rev. J. A. Sligh	2	21	7	5	8	1				400	8	6		3	20	125	5 00	10 00	16 80	20 00		65 00	630 00	250 00	10
Rev. J. D. Bowles	3	23	5	12	2	3				387	1	7	6	2	9	110	10 00	22 60		36 65			950 00	199 75	11
Rev. J. D. Shirey	1	7	13	10	9	8				226	3		1	2	8	40	32 25	8 35	2 00	7 35		4 75	225 00	600 00	12
Rev. S. Bonknight	1	3	4	21	3	7				240	1	5		2	10	75	25 00	15 00		35 00	5 00	187 00	500 00	150 00	13
Rev. J. F. Probst	1		2		2					130		3	3	1	16	125	35 00	16 00	6 25	15 00		175 00	1290 00	125 00	14
Rev. H. W. Kuhns	1	6	4	5		4				130	3	4	4	1	8	70	14 25	5 00		10 00	10 00	70 00	430 00		
Rev. Z. W. Bedenbaugh	1	1	2	6		2			1	83	1	5	5	1	11	80	5 00	5				475 00	840 00		
Rev. G. A. Hough	1	5		4						104		2	2	1	14	100	5 00	5 00					275 00	121 0	
Rev. E. Caughman	1	3	3	2	3					160	1	1	1	1	6	30	6 25					200 00	60 00		
Rev. J. B. Haskell*	1	13	1	4		1				39	2			2	8	50	2 10	12 55		22 85		224 30	500 00	37 50	
Rev. W. S. Bowman, D. D.	1	1		4		9	2			42	1	4		1	12	38				150 00		1376 96	1500 00	30 00	
Rev. E. T. Horn	1	51	1	29	9	7		1		277		21		1	35	265	36 00				60 00		200 00		
Rev. L. Muller, D. D.	1	86		52	7		2			345	9		2	1	30	180							1800 00		
Orangeburg Conference	1	2			120		1			500 18		82	1	1	40 5	450 27		5 00				57 00			
Totals	46	386 63	63	906	176	176 50	12	11 3	3	5314 47	47	192 35 47	35	47	369	2840	$407 85	$200 55	$36 05	$412 60	$75 00	$4468 87	$15411 00	$3675 37	

* Six Months Service.

MEMOIRS.

REV. SAMUEL BOUKNIGHT

After having filled important positions in Church and State, passed away at his residence near Leesville, Lexington County, S. C., on the 30th June, 1876, lacking but a few months of surviving out the time allotted to mortals in this life.

Brought up in the Lutheran Church, he was quite early impressed with the idea of joining the Christian Ministry, and in his 27th year made application for the privilege of a licentiate, which was granted by the Synod, then sitting in St. Matthew's, Orangeburg Co. In laboring as a licentiate, he did incalculable good, besides laying broad and deep those foundations, which, in after time, proved to be the secret of his success in pointing sinners to the Lamb of God. During the time he grounded himself thoroughly and profoundly, not only in the fundamental doctrines and principles of his own Church, but also the faiths and creeds of other Churches. He loved truth wherever it could be found, and the Church to which he belonged did not sectionalize his mind to that extent as to make him fail to appreciate in others the truth as it was found in the Gospel. The Lutheran Church at the time of his entrance, was among the weakest in the State, and it labored among many trials and heavy burdens. He shared with its hardships, he toiled zealously for it interests, and lived for its promotion throughout the bounds of the State. In those Counties were Lutheranism was known only in name, there he went as a pioneer, and among a few followers, planted the colors of a Church. The prosperous days of St. Mark's of the Saluda. the vigorous christian growth of St. Peters, the faithful activity of the Leesville Chapel, among many others were the results of the ministerial labors of our esteemed Bro. Bouknight. His mind was vigorous, his conception of all subjects was clear and accurate, and his judgment of men and their actions sound and reliable. His life was like all human lives, checkered, but he like the good man always does, bent circumstances to the service of God. He viewed lifes ills as mere incidents, and instead of letting them rule him he ruled them. As a neighbor he was ever thoughtful and warm-hearted, as a husband he was respected and loved, to many sad hearts he was a ministering angel, to others he stood in the capacity of a father. But he has finished his course, and fought the "good fight" with the heroism of the christian gladiator, and winning the "Eternal weight of glory" the sought for prize, he has gone to take his place among his companions the angels.

J. H. BAILEY,
Chairman Committee on Memoirs.

REV. JESSE B. LOWMAN

Was born in Lexington Co., S. C., in the year 1814. He entered the Theological Seminary at Lexington in 1845 ; graduated in 1848; was licensed to preach the gospel on the 22d of November of the same year; was fully ordained to the Gospel Ministry at Ebenezer, Effingham Co., Ga., in 1851, and departed this life by a sad casualty on the 25th day of February, 1875, in the 62 year of his age.

Of a modest and unassuming disposition he sought neither notoriety nor the praise of men, but labored zealously, earnestly, and untiringly, from no other motive, and with no other object in view than a disinterested love of souls, and an earnest desire for the building up of the Redeemer's Kingdom. He never could be induced to extend his labors beyond his native County, but found constant and profitable employment in building up the waste places, and gathering together and ministering to the scattered membership of our Church in Lexington County, and in these labors he was eminently blessed, for he laid the foundation of some of the most flourishing congregations of Lexington Co. His preaching was simple, but characterized by earnestness and sincere love of souls—its aim being to reach the heart and to persuade men to become reconciled to God.

During his Ministry he served at different times nearly every congregation in Lexington, of some of them he was the founder, whose growth and prosperity under his care, amply compensated him for his self-denying labors. He was always welcomed among his people, with almost parental love, for he had always a word of comfort for the sorrowing, and encouragement for the youthful christian. In his intercourse with his christian brethren, he was genial and affable—with the world, he was courtious and respectful, but ever ready, in kindness to reprove, rebuke, and admonish. The great purposes of his life were to know nothing but Christ and to preach Christ only, and him crucified, and at the resurrection many will hail him as the instrument of their salvation. He fell at the post of duty, and ere this has heard the *"well done good and faithful servant"* of his Lord.

JAS. H. BAILEY,
Chairman Committee on Memoirs.

MINUTES OF THE MINISTERIUM.

FIRST SESSION.

St. Stephen's Church,
Lexington C. H., S. C., Oct. 11, 1876.

The Ministerium met at four o'clock, P. M., and was opened with prayer by Rev. H. W. Kuhns.

On motion it was,

Resolved, That the application of Mr. S. P. Hughes for ordination be received.

Resolved, That the examination of Mr. Hughes take place before the Ministerium at four o'clock, P. M., to-morrow.

Adjourned with benediction by the President.

SECOND SESSION.

Oct. 12th, 1876.

The Ministerium met at 4 o'clock, P. M., and was opened with prayer by Rev. B. F. Berry.

On motion it was,

Resolved, That Mr. J. P. Hawkins be received as a beneficiary on the funds of this Synod.

Resolved, That a Committee be appointed to examine Mr. M. O. J. Kreps, and if the examination prove satisfactory, that he be recommended to the Committee on appropriations.

Resolved, That the business of the hour be taken up. Pending the examination, Ministerium adjourned to meet at 4 o'clock to morrow.

Benediction by Rev. J. D. Shirey.

THIRD SESSION.

Oct. 13th 1876, 4 o'clock, P. M.

The Ministerium met, and was opened with prayer by Rev. D. Kyser.

Minutes 'of the previous session were read and approved.

A fraternal letter was received from Rev. Dr. Muller, of Charleston, a member of this Ministerium, and the Corresponding Secretary was instructed to reply to this letter heartily reciprocating his fraternal sentiments and explaining the matter of his request. The business of the hour was resumed and prosecuted for a while, pending which the Ministerium adjourned.

Benediction by the President.

FOURTH SESSION.

OCT. 14, 1876, 6 o'clock, P. M.

Ministerium met, and was opened with prayer by Rev. J. Hawkins.

The Committee on Examination reported as follows:

Your Committee desires to report that it has had two interviews with Bro. S. P. Hughes, in the presence of this Body, and that so far as our examination has extended, it has proved satisfactory. We take pleasure in recommending that he be ordained to the Holy office of the Ministry, at such time as this Ministerium may designate.   Respectfully submitted,

J. P. SMELTZER,
W. S. BOWMAN,
J. H. HONOUR,
J. D. SHIREY.

Adopted.

Resolved, That the Ordination sermon be preached on to-morrow at 11 o'clock, A. M., and that Bro. Hughes be ordained to the office of the Holy Ministry immediately after the close of the sermon.

Resolved, That Revs. W. S. Bowman, D. D., J. P. Smeltzer, D. D., H. W. Kuhns, J. Hawkins and H. S. Wingard be appointed a Standing Committee on Examination of candidates for ordination, and that it shall be the duty of the President to fill any vacancies by appointment that may hereafter occur by removal or otherwise.

Resolved, That a Committee consisting of Revs. J. F. Probst and J. P. Smeltzer, D. D., be appointed by this Ministerium to confer with Rev. A. W. Lindler, with reference to his application for dismission from this Synod.

Rev. J. Hawkins was chosen to preach the sermon on Education at the next meeting of Synod, and Rev. J. P. Smeltzer, D. D., his Alternate.

Rev. J. D. Shirey to preach the Ordination Sermon at next meeting of Synod, and Rev. J. A. Sligh his Alternate.

Ministerium adjourned.

Benediction by Rev. A. L. Crouse.

CORNELIUS P. BOOZER,

Recording Secretary of Ministerium.

OFFICERS OF SYNOD.

Rev. Edwin A. Bolles, President.............. *Columbia, S. C.*
Rev. W. S. Bowman, D. D., Vice-President...... *Charleston, S. C.*
Rev. C. P. Boozer, Recording Secretary.......... *Leesville, S. C.*
Rev. H. W. Kuhns, Corresponding Secretary..... *Newberry, S. C.*
Maj. P. E. Wise, Treasurer of Synod............ *Prosperity, S. C.*
Mr. J. F. Schirmer, Treasurer Seminary Fund.... *Charleston, S. C.*
Mr. T. W. Holloway, Treasurer Widows Fund.... *Pomaria, S. C.*
Mr. U. B. Whites, Treasurer Missionary Fund.... *Prosperity, S. C.*
Mr. O. L. Schumpert, Treas. Endowment Fund... *Newberry, S. C.*

EXECUTIVE COMMITTEE OF MISSIONARY SOCIETY.

Rev. H. W. Kuhns,	Mr. W. W. Houseal,
Rev. J. A. Sligh,	O. L. Schumpert, Esq.,
Rev. H. S. Wingard,	Mr. U. B. Whites,
Mr. H. S. Boozer.	

STANDING RESOLUTION.

Resolved, That hereafter any Minister accepting of a charge within our bounds, shall not, under penalty of being centured by Synod, enter upon his labor until the charge shall have made a satisfactory settlement with their former Pastor, and that this shall be considered the standing rule among us, and printed on the face of our Minutes from year to year.

www.ingramcontent.com/pod-product-compliance
Lightning Source LLC
Chambersburg PA
CBHW022039080426
42733CB00007B/892